KINGFISHER
READERS

Animal Colors

Thea Feldman

KINGFISHER
NEW YORK

KINGFISHER
LONDON & NEW YORK

Copyright © Kingfisher 2014
Published in the United States and Canada by Kingfisher,
175 Fifth Ave., New York, NY 10010
Kingfisher is an imprint of Macmillan Children's Books, London.
All rights reserved.

Distributed in the U.S. by Macmillan,
175 Fifth Ave., New York, NY 10010

Library of Congress Cataloging-in-Publication data
has been applied for.

Series editor: Thea Feldman
Literacy consultant: Ellie Costa, Bank Street School for Children, New York

978-0-7534-7134-0 (HB)
978-0-7534-7135-7 (PB)

Kingfisher books are available for special promotions
and premiums. For details contact: Special Markets
Department, Macmillan, 175 Fifth Ave.,
New York, NY 10010.

For more information, please visit
www.kingfisherbooks.com

Printed in China
9 8 7 6 5 4 3 2 1
1TR/0713/WKT/UG/115MA

Picture credits
The Publisher would like to thank the following for permission to reproduce their
material. Every care has been taken to trace copyright holders. However, if there
have been unintentional omissions or failure to trace copyright holders, we apologize
and will, if informed, endeavor to make corrections in any future edition.

Top = t; Bottom = b; Center = c; Left = l; Right = r
Cover Steve Parish/Steve Parish Publishing/Corbis; 3 Shutterstock/chrom; 4 FLPA/Piotr Naskrecki/
Minden Pictures; 5 Shutterstock/Yellowj; 6t FLPA/Ingo Arndt/Minden Pictures;
6b Shutterstock; 7t; FLPA/moomsabuy; 7b FLPA/Fabio Pupin; 8 FLPA/Michael Breuer/Biosphoto;
9 Shutterstock/Neale Cousland; 10t Shutterstock/Jason S.; 10b Shutterstock/Mogens Trolle;
11t Shutterstock/Hung Chung Chih; 11b FLPA/Norbert Probst/Imagebroker; 12l Shutterstock/
Serg64; 12r Shutterstock/Eric Isselee; 13t Shutterstock/Khoroshunova Olga; 13b Shutterstock/Eric
Isselee; 14l Shutterstock/ romanvm66; 14c Shutterstock/Eric Isselee; 15t Shutterstock/bmaki;
15b Shutterstock/stockshotportfolio; 16–17 FLPA/Alfred Schauhuber/Imagebroker;
18 Shutterstock/Eduard Kyslynskyy; 19 FLPA/Bernd Rohrschneider; 20 Shutterstock/Ian Grainger;
21 Shutterstock/Sue Robinson; 22 FLPA/Bernd Rohrschneider; 23 FLPA/Thorsten Negro/
Imagebroker; 24t Shutterstock/Alfredo Maiquez; 24b Shutterstock/ Kletr; 25t Shutterstock/Brandon
Alms; 25b Shutterstock/Dirk Ercken; 26 Shutterstock/Steve McWilliam; 27 Shutterstock/James
Coleman; 28 FLPA/Thomas Marent/Minden Pictures; 29 Shutterstock/apiguide; 30t Shutterstock/
worldswildlifewonders; 30bl FLPA/GTW/Imagebroker; 31t Shutterstock/Dobermaraner;
31b Shutterstock/Marty Wakat.

There are many colorful animals in the world!

This grasshopper is bright green.

This snake is green too.

These birds are pink.

This crab is red.

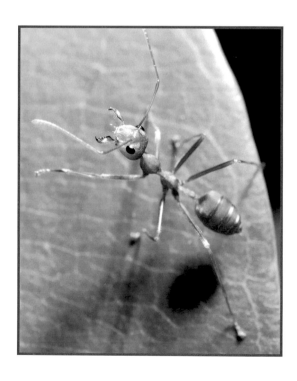

So is
this ant.

This sea star
is blue.

So is this lizard.

This bear is brown
from its head to its tail.

It is all one color.

Some animals are
more than one color.

How many different
colors do you see
on this bird?

Some animals are
black and white.

Some animals
have spots.

Some animals
have stripes.

The colors of some animals
help them hide
from other animals.

This is called **camouflage**
(say CAM-uh-flahj).

This brown **hare** hides
from animals that hunt.

Its fur helps the hare
blend in with the grass
and the ground.

Do you see it?

A tiger is a hunter.

It has black and orange stripes.

A tiger's stripes help it
hide in tall grass.

The tiger hides until
an animal comes near.

Then the tiger will jump
out to catch it!

Some animals change
their colors!

This spider is white
when it is on a white flower.

It turns yellow on a
yellow flower.

Insects do not see the spider.

The spider grabs and eats
this insect!

Sometimes this chameleon
(say ka-MEE-lee-yun)
is green.

Now it is red and white!

The chameleon can change colors in about 20 seconds.

The colors of some animals say "Stay away from me!"

These tiny frogs have **poison** in them.

Their bright
colors tell
other animals
"I taste bad!"

Other animals do not
eat the frogs.

The red on this
moth lets other
animals know it is
not good to eat.

A skunk's white stripes
say "Go away!"

The colors of some animals help them find **mates**.

This male lizard's orange neck says "Here I am!"

The bright color helps female lizards find him.

This male peacock has
bright tail feathers.

Females look for males
with the brightest feathers.

Which color
do you like
the best?

Do you see an animal
that color in this book?

Glossary

blend to mix in with other things of the same color and be hard to see, such as a brown hare in front of earth or rocks

camouflage when an animal's colors helps it hide from other animals

hare a furry animal with long ears that looks a lot like a rabbit

mate an animal that gets together with another animal to have babies

poison something that some animals make that can kill other animals